'BRARY
d to a
or
D0491748

# JAMAICA

LETTERS FROM AROUND THE WORLD

# Ali Brownlie

### Photographs by Sue Cunningham

BwD Library Services

3 0303 00434 0545

LETTERS FROM AROUND THE WORLD

## Titles in this series

# AUSTRALIA · BANGLADESH · BRAZIL · CANADA · CHINA
# COSTA RICA · EGYPT · FRANCE · GERMANY · GREECE · INDIA
# INDONESIA · IRELAND · ITALY · JAMAICA · JAPAN · KENYA
# MEXICO · NIGERIA · PAKISTAN · POLAND · RUSSIA
# SAUDI ARABIA · SOUTH AFRICA · SPAIN · SWEDEN · THE USA

A Cherrytree Book

Conceived and produced by

Nutshell
MEDIA

www.nutshellmedialtd.co.uk

First published in paperback in 2009 by
Evans Brothers Ltd
2A Portman Mansions
Chiltern Street
London W1U 6NR

VISIT OUR WEBSITE
Evans
www.evansbooks.co.uk

Editor: Polly Goodman
Design: Mayer Media Ltd
Map artwork: Encompass Graphics Ltd
All other artwork: Mayer Media Ltd

All photographs were taken by Sue Cunningham.

Acknowledgements
The author and photographer would like to thank the
Buck family, the staff and pupils of Esher Primary School,
Jamaica, and Claudette Salmon for all their help with
this book.

All Rights Reserved. No part of this publication may be
reproduced, stored in a retrieval system or transmitted in
any form, electronic, mechanical, photocopying, record-
ing or otherwise, without the prior permission of Evans
Brothers Limited. © Copyright Evans Brothers 2003

British Library Cataloguing in Publication Data
Brownlie, Alison, 1949-
    Jamaica – (Letters from around the world)
    1. Jamaica – Social conditions – 20th century –
    Juvenile literature
    2. Jamaica – Social life and customs – 20th century –
    Juvenile literature
    I. Title
    972.9'2'06

ISBN-13: 978-1842345818

Cover: Travis (second from the right) with his friends
  Davian, Junior and Jason, in their school uniform.
Title page: Travis (centre), Davian and Jason messing
  about in the sea.
This page: The beach at Negril.
Contents page: Travis and his friends with their catch.
Glossary page: Travis in a maths lesson at school.
Further Information page: Playing football after school.
Index: Travis covers his friend Jason with sand.

BLACKBURN WITH
DARWEN LIBRARY

004340545

| Bertrams | 22/04/2009 |
| J917.292FR | £7.99 |

# Contents

# My Country

Monday, 5 March

Green Island
Negril-Montego Bay Road
Jamaica

Dear Sam,

My name is Travis Buck and I'm 9 years old. I live near a small village called Green Island. It's on the island of Jamaica, in the Caribbean Sea. I have two elder brothers, Nick and Max, and one younger sister, Whitney. Our grandparents live with us, too. Do you have any brothers or sisters? I can't wait to get a letter from you.

Catch you later!

From

## Travis

This is me with my mum, dad, brothers, sister, cousin and grandma. We're on the veranda of our house. ➡

Jamaica is the third-largest
island in the Caribbean Sea. Only
Cuba and Hispaniola are bigger.

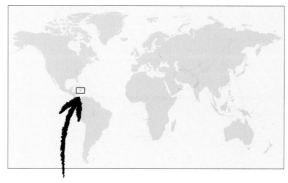

Jamaica's place in the world.

CARIBBEAN SEA

Montego Bay
Lucea
Green Island
Negril
Savanna-la-Mar

Black River

JAMAICA

Blue Mountain Peak
2,256m

Spanish Town
Portmore

KINGSTON

Port Antonio

Great Pedro Bluff

Portland Point

CARIBBEAN SEA

N

0   20   40   60 kilometres
0      20        40 miles

Jamaica was a British colony for about 300 years.
It became independent in 1962. Kingston is the
capital and also the biggest city.

Green Island is not really an island. It is a small village by the sea, on the west coast of Jamaica. The busy main road between Montego Bay and Negril passes through Green Island.

The beautiful beach at Negril attracts tourists as well as local people.

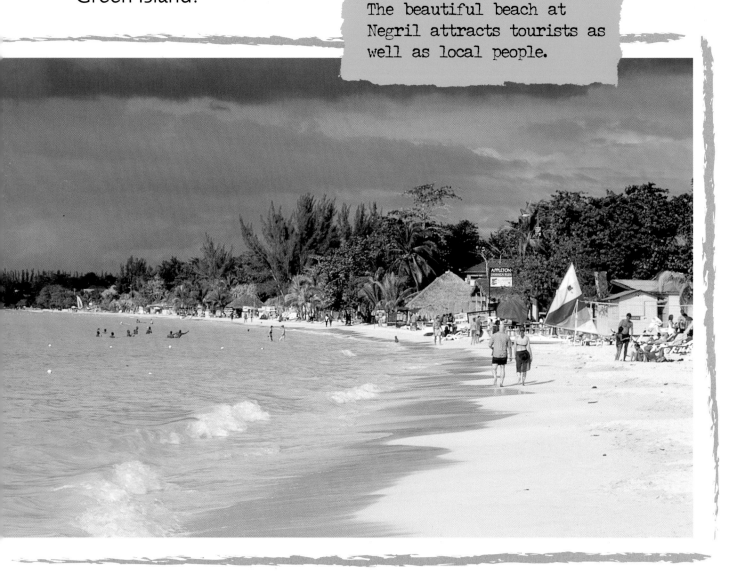

Negril is a popular holiday resort about 10 kilometres away from Green Island. Tourists visit Negril from all over the world.

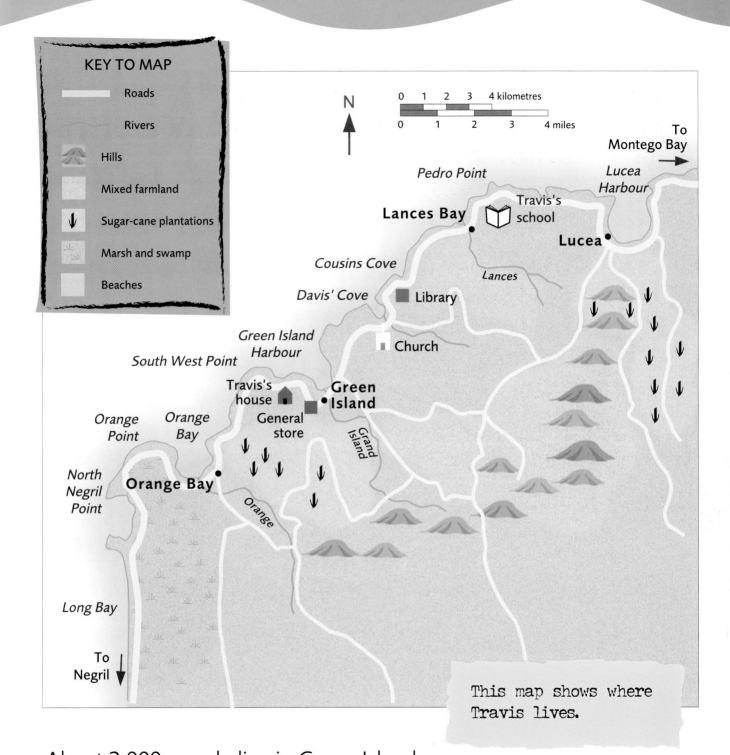

**KEY TO MAP**

| | |
|---|---|
| Roads | |
| Rivers | |
| Hills | |
| Mixed farmland | |
| Sugar-cane plantations | |
| Marsh and swamp | |
| Beaches | |

N

0  1  2  3  4 kilometres

0  1  2  3  4 miles

To Montego Bay

Pedro Point

Lucea Harbour

**Lances Bay**

Travis's school

**Lucea**

Cousins Cove

Lances

Davis' Cove

Library

Green Island Harbour

Church

South West Point

Travis's house

**Green Island**

General store

Grand Island

Orange Point

Orange Bay

North Negril Point

**Orange Bay**

Orange

Long Bay

To Negril

This map shows where Travis lives.

About 2,000 people live in Green Island.
There is one general store, a church and a library.
The general store sells most things that people
need from day to day. If they need anything
special, they have to drive to Montego Bay.

# Landscape and Weather

Green Island is surrounded by plantations and other farmland. A short way inland there is a ridge of low hills covered with trees. Many colourful birds live there, such as hummingbirds.

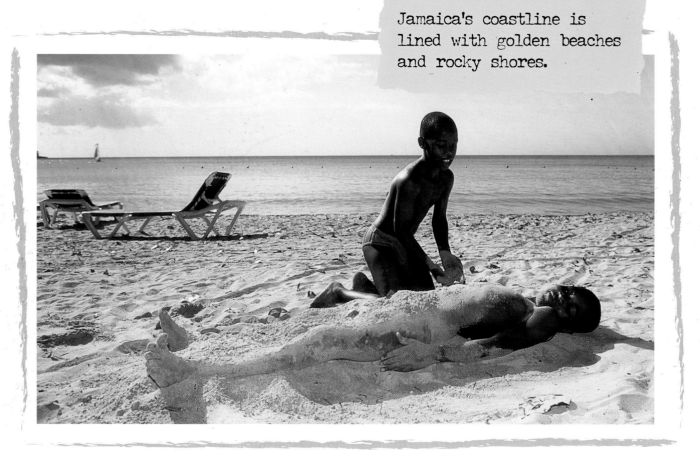

Jamaica's coastline is lined with golden beaches and rocky shores.

Like the rest of Jamaica, Green Island is hot all year round. Between May and October it can rain heavily in short, sharp bursts. But for the rest of the year, there is very little rain. Sometimes there are hurricanes in September or October.

Tropical fruits such as bananas, mangoes and breadfruit grow well in Jamaica's hot climate.

### Jamaica's Climate

| January | July |
| --- | --- |
| Temperature | Temperature |
| 30°C | 32°C |
| 46mm | 147mm |
| Rainfall | Rainfall |

# At Home

Travis's house is made from bricks and concrete. His aunt's house (right) is older. It is made from wood.

Travis's house is on a plot of four houses, where his aunts, uncles and cousins all live. They spend a lot of time visiting each other's houses.

Ackee is a fruit that grows in Travis's garden. It is part of Jamaica's national dish, ackee and salt fish.

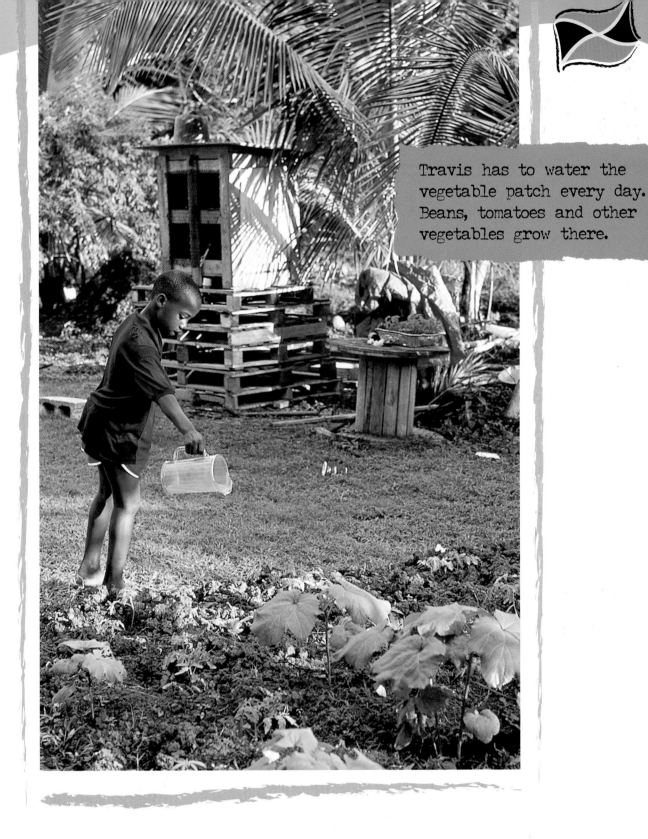

Travis has to water the vegetable patch every day. Beans, tomatoes and other vegetables grow there.

Travis's house has four bedrooms, a kitchen/living-room and a bathroom, all on one floor. There is a big garden, where the family grows its own vegetables.

Travis chooses a music CD to listen to.

Travis likes listening to music on the CD player and watching TV. His favourite music is reggae, which started in Jamaica.

In the evening, the family likes to sit out on the veranda. Most Jamaican houses have a veranda.

Travis shares a bedroom with his brothers. The fan keeps them cool at night.

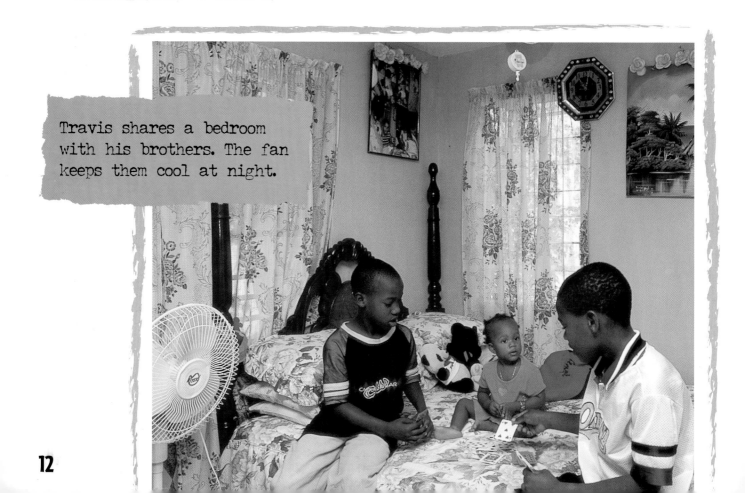

Wednesday, 7 May

Green Island
Negril-Montego Bay Road
Jamaica

Hi Sam,

How's it going? It was hard work here yesterday because our water supply was cut off. Workmen were mending the road near our house when they hit a water pipe that goes under the road. It's the second time in a month! I had to collect water straight from the pipe and carry it back to the house. We need water for cooking, washing and drinking so I had to make five trips. Does your water or power ever get cut off?

From

# Travis

Collecting the water was hot work but the water kept my feet cool!

# Food and Mealtimes

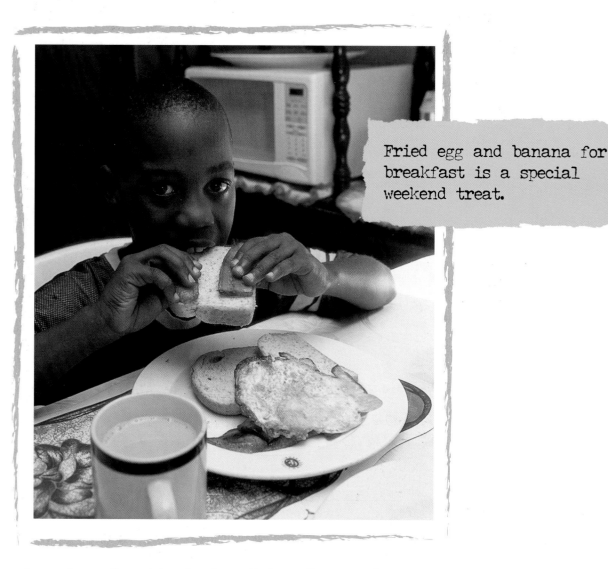

Fried egg and banana for breakfast is a special weekend treat.

Jamaican food includes dishes from other countries. This is because people from all over the world have come to live in Jamaica.

For breakfast, Travis usually has a cup of tea and some fruit. Sometimes he has fried egg or fried banana.

In the evening, the family often eats chicken, rice and peas cooked in coconut milk. Sometimes they have bammy, which is fried bread eaten with fried fish. On special occasions they have curried goat.

Jerk chicken is a spicy Jamaican dish. It is often sold from stands in the street.

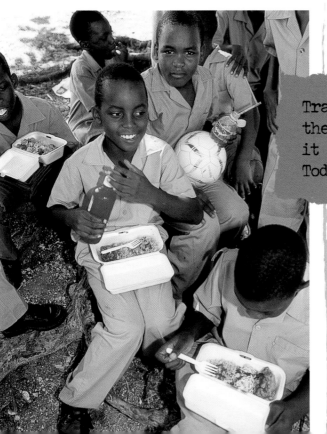

Travis buys his lunch from the school canteen and eats it outside with his friends. Today it's chicken and rice.

Monday, 20 July

Green Island
Negril-Montego Bay Road
Jamaica

Hello there!

Thanks for the recipe you sent me. Here's one for you. It's for Jamaica's national dish – ackee and salt fish.

You will need: 250g salt fish, 1 tin of ackee (you can find salted cod and tinned ackee in international food stores), 3 tablespoons of groundnut oil, 1 large onion, 1 large tomato, $1/2$ green chilli (deseeded and chopped), black pepper

In Jamaica we use fresh ackee, but it will be easier for you to buy it in a tin.

1. Rinse the salt fish and leave it soaking in water overnight.
2. Chop the onion, tomato and pepper.
3. Heat the fish in fresh water and simmer for 10 minutes.

The ackee is added to the salt fish.

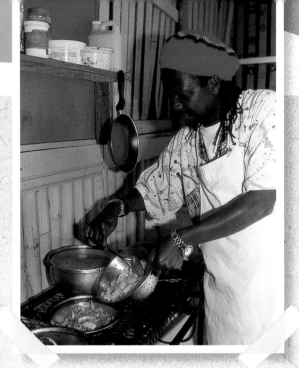

4. Let the fish cool down and flake it into small pieces with a fork. Make sure there are no bones in it.

5. Heat the oil in a large frying pan (Mum always does that for me.)

6. Fry the onions, pepper and tomato until the onions are soft.

7. Add the ackee and fish, and cook for another 5 minutes.

8. Add black pepper and serve.

Write and tell me what you think!

From

# Travis

The ackee and salt fish are nearly ready. The dish will look a bit like scrambled egg when it is finished.

# School Day

Travis goes to Esher Primary School, which is 10 kilometres away. His dad usually drives him there in his taxi. Other children get there by minibus, which they flag down like a taxi. The school day starts with assembly at 8 a.m.

At assembly, all the children line up outside their classroom while their teacher calls the register.

There are 25 children in Travis's class. Displays of their work are on the classroom walls.

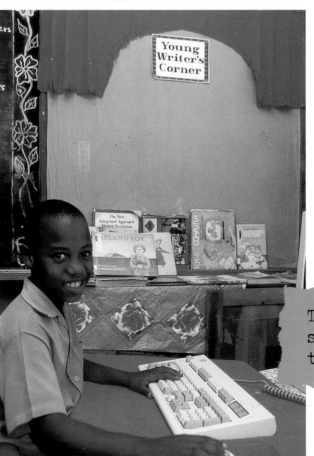

In Jamaica, all children start school at the age of 6. When he is 12, Travis will take an exam called the National Assessment Programme. If he passes this he can go to secondary school.

Travis practises writing stories on the computer in the school library.

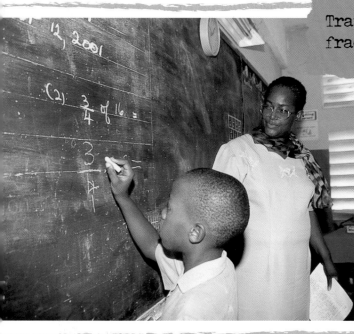

Travis shows how to do fractions on the chalkboard.

Travis's class learns maths, English, science, social studies, art, geography and sport. The school day finishes at 3 p.m., but Travis often stays on after school to play football with his friends.

Travis and his friends play football on a makeshift pitch outside the school.

Thursday, 15 August

Green Island
Negril-Montego Bay Road
Jamaica

Hey Sam!

I'm glad you liked the recipe I sent you.

Did I tell you about our end-of-term concert? Everyone at school has to put on a performance, either play some music, act in a play, or dance. I belong to a band and we're practising real hard. We made our drums out of big tins and I played a home-made wooden flute. We'd better win this year.

What do you do at the end of term?

Write soon!

# Travis

This is me (on the right) practising with my band.

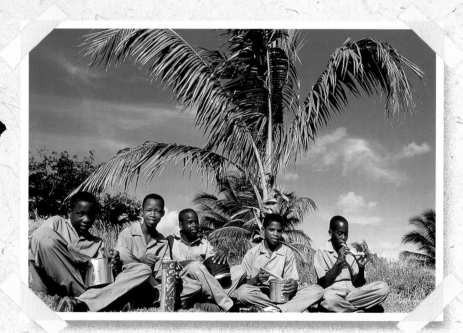

# Off to Work

In the past, most people from Green Island worked on sugar-cane plantations nearby. There are still some plantations, but most of them have closed down. People had to find different jobs.

These miners are off to work at a bauxite mine. Jamaica is one of the world's biggest suppliers of bauxite.

Days on the sugar-cane plantations are long, hot and hard.

Many people from the village now work in hotels and restaurants, in holiday resorts like Negril and Montego Bay. Travis's dad is a taxi driver. Many of his customers are tourists.

This woman works in a tourist office. She helps tourists find somewhere to stay and places to visit.

# Free Time

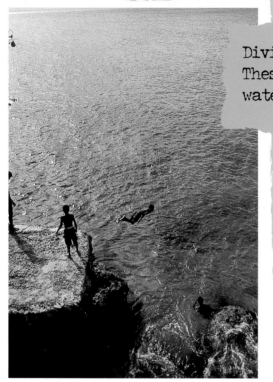

Diving from the rocks is great fun. These boys have made sure that the water is deep enough first.

Travis spends every weekend down by the sea. Swimming, diving and fishing are all favourite sports. He has been on holiday to Kingston with his family, but he has never been abroad.

Travis and his friends caught this fish by wading into the sea and grabbing it with their hands.

Saturday, 8 September

Green Island
Negril-Montego Bay Road
Jamaica

Hi Sam,

You asked how to play draughts. Here's how we play it:

1. Choose who will have the white counters and who will have the black. Line them up on opposite sides of the board, on the black squares of the back rows.

2. Start by moving one counter at a time. You only play on the black squares, and each counter can only move diagonally.

3. If your counter is next to your opponent's counter, and the square beyond it is free, you can 'jump' over it and remove the counter from the board.

4. The winner is the first person to remove all their opponent's counters.

From

# Travis

You have to think ahead when playing draughts. ➔

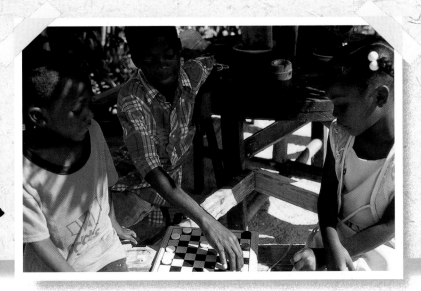

# Religion and Festivals

Most people in Jamaica are Christians. There are Rastafarians, Hindus and Muslims, too. As well as Christmas and Easter, Jamaicans have holidays to celebrate their history and their freedom from slavery.

Churches are usually packed on a Sunday. People join in the service with singing and clapping.

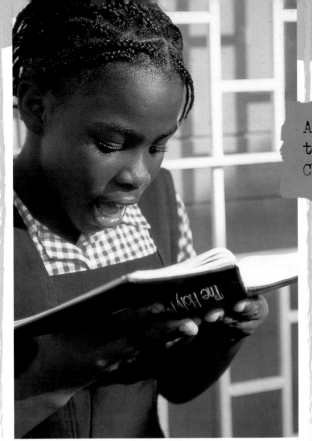

At school, children learn to read the Bible, the Christian holy book.

Jamaicans celebrate Christmas in their own special way. Christmas carols are sung with a reggae beat. There is lots of music and parades, and plenty to eat.

Many children go to Sunday school, where they learn stories from the Bible.

# Fact File

**Capital city:** The capital of Jamaica is Kingston, which has a population of 700,000. Kingston is a major port.

**Population:** Just over 2.8 million people live in Jamaica.

**Size:** 11,000km$^2$. Jamaica is the third-largest island in the Caribbean.

**Flag:** The Jamaican flag has three colours. Black stands for the hardships Jamaican people had to face in the past. Gold stands for the sun. Green stands for the land and hope for the future.

**Motto:** 'Out of many, one.' This means out of many different people from all over the world, Jamaica is one nation of people.

**Currency:** Jamaican dollar. There are 100 cents in a Jamaican dollar.

**Main industries:** Tourism, bauxite, sugar, bananas and coffee.

**Language:** Jamaica's official language is English, but most people speak Jamaican patois, which is a combination of English, Spanish, Portuguese and African languages.

**Main religions:** Over 80 per cent of Jamaicans are Christians. There are also many Rastafarians.

**Highest mountain:** Blue Mountain Peak (2,256m). Coffee is grown on the slopes of the surrounding mountains.

**Longest river:** The Black River is 53km long.

**Wildlife:** The Black River is famous for its crocodiles. They live to be over 100 years old. The national bird is the hummingbird. The national flower is the tree of life.

**Famous people:** Bob Marley was a famous singer, guitarist and composer of reggae music. He died in 1981 aged just 36. Linford Christie was born in Jamaica in 1960 and went to live in England as a boy. By 1993 he held the World, Olympic, Commonwealth and European Cup titles for running the 100 metres. Marcus Garvey was born in 1887 and campaigned for freedom for black people, both in Jamaica and in the USA. He died in 1940 and is buried in the National Heroes Park, in Kingston.

**Stamps:** Jamaican stamps often show famous Jamaican people, such as Bob Marley. Other stamps show wildlife, sport or scenes in history.

# Glossary

**ackee** A type of fruit that was originally grown in West Africa. It is poisonous if it is not ripe.

**bauxite** A metal used to make aluminium.

**breadfruit** A large fruit, weighing up to 5kg, which is often roasted.

**colony** A country owned and controlled by another country.

**Equator** An imaginary line that runs around the middle of the Earth.

**hurricane** A very severe storm with strong winds and heavy rain.

**jerk chicken** Chicken that has been soaked in spices and barbecued.

**plantation** A large farm where only one crop is grown.

**Rastafarian** Someone who follows the Rastafarian religion, a Jamaican religion which began in Ethiopia. Rastafarians are vegetarian.

**reggae** A type of music that is very popular in Jamaica. It has a heavy, off-beat rhythm.

**resort** A place where people go on holiday.

**salt fish** Cod that has been salted and dried to preserve it.

**slavery** Many of the ancestors of people in Jamaica were brought over from Africa as slaves. They had to work hard for the people who bought them.

**sugar-cane** Tall grass which contains sugar in its sap.

**tourism** The business of providing services to holidaymakers.

**tropical** Between the Tropics of Cancer and Capricorn on the world map. Tropical areas have hot, wet weather all year round.

**veranda** A porch along the outside of a building. Many houses in hot countries have verandas.

# Further Information

## Information books:

*The Changing Face of the Caribbean* by Ali Brownlie Bojang (Wayland, 2006)

*Facts About Countries: The Caribbean* by Ian Graham (Franklin Watts, 2005)

*Festivals and Food: The Caribbean* by Linda Illsley (Wayland, 2006)

*Festivals of the World: Jamaica* (Franklin Watts, 2006)

*Food Around the World: The Caribbean* by Polly Goodman (Wayland, 2006)

*Living in Jamaica* by Judy Bastyra (Franklin Watts, 2005)

*Looking at Countries: The Caribbean* by Jillian Powell (Franklin Watts, 2006)

*My Caribbean Family History* by Vic Parker (Heinemann, 2007)

*Welcome to My Country: Jamaica* by K. Kwek and J. Haque (Franklin Watts, 2005)

## Poetry and fiction:

*A Caribbean Dozen: Poems from Caribbean Poets* by John Agard and Grace Nichols (Walker, 2007)

*Sing Me a Story: Song and Dance Stories from the Caribbean* by Grace Hallworth (Frances Lincoln, 2003)

*Traditional Stories From The Caribbean* by Petronella Breinburg (Wayland, 2006)

*Traditional Tales From The Caribbean* by Vic Parker (Chrysalis Children's Books, 2004)

*Under The Moon And Over The Sea: A Collection Of Caribbean Poems* by John Agard and Grace Nichols (Walker, 2007)

# Index